Spot the difference
THINGS THAT GO!

© 2022 Webber Books

All rights reserved. This book or any portion thereof may not be reproduced or used in any manner whatsoever without the express written permission of the publisher except for the use of brief quotations in a book review.

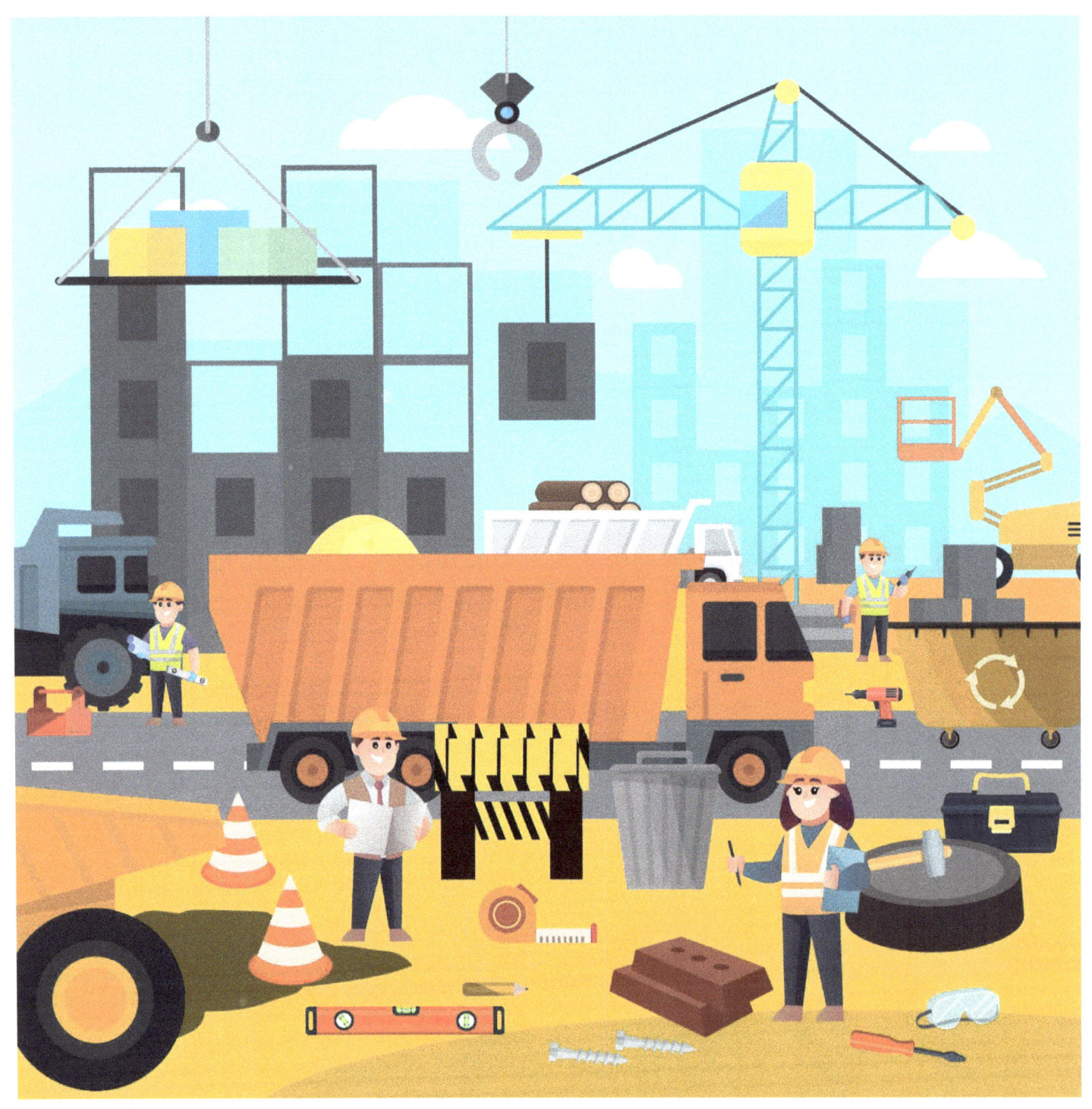

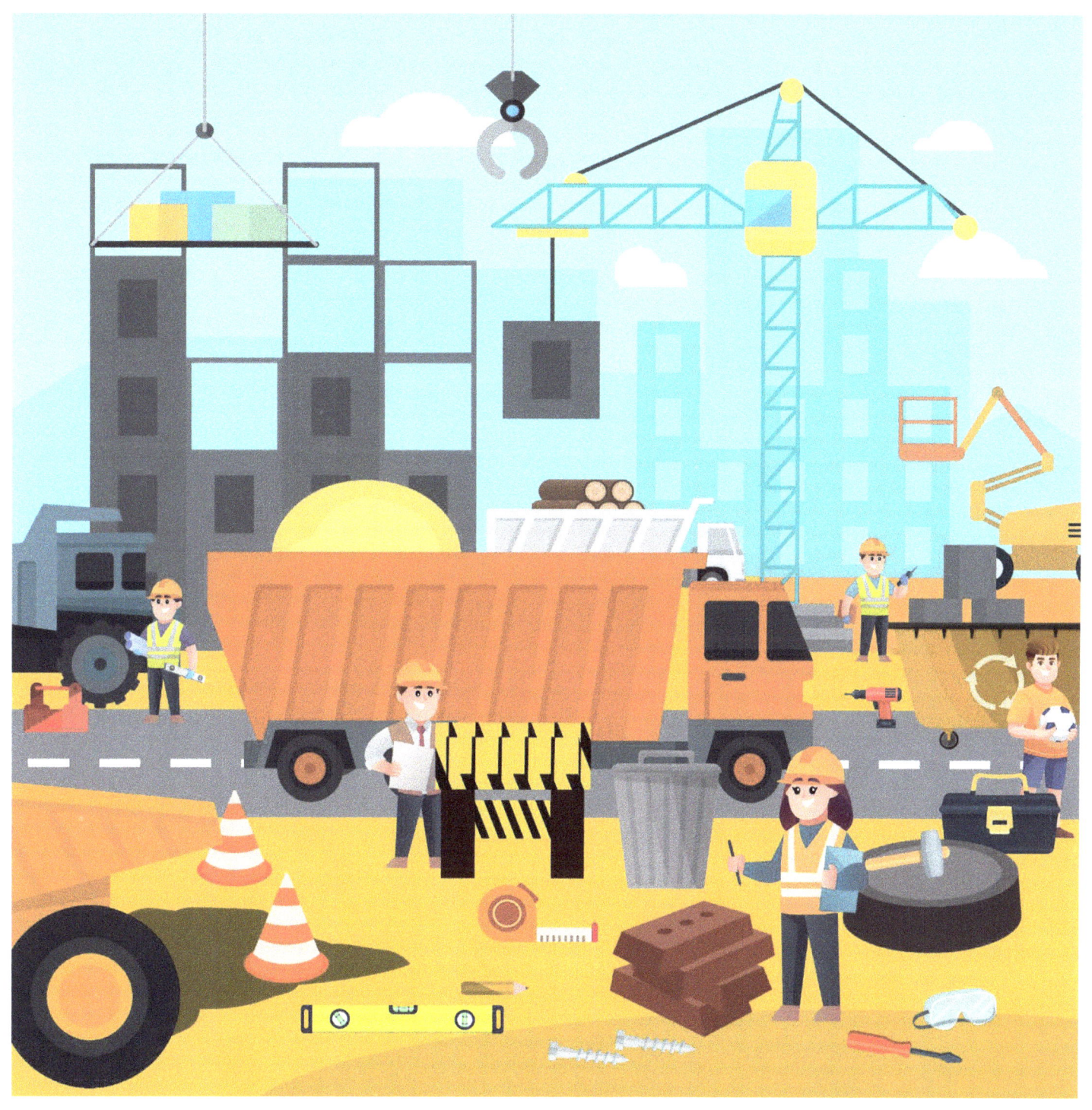

CAN YOU SPOT THE **7** DIFFERENCES...?

IT'S TIME TO BOARD THE AIRPORT PLANE!

CAN YOU SPOT THE 7 DIFFERENCES...?

THIS PARK LOOKS WHEELY WHEELY NICE!

CAN YOU SPOT THE 8 DIFFERENCES...?

IT'S RUSH HOUR ON THESE BUSY ROADS!

ARR... A PIRATE SHIP HAS COME TO SHORE!

THE BREAKDOWN TRUCK SAVES THE DAY!

WHOOSH! ROCKETS GO SUPER DUPER FAST!

CAN YOU SPOT THE 9 DIFFERENCES...?

YAY! THE FOOD TRUCKS HAVE COME TO TOWN!

CAN YOU SPOT THE 9 DIFFERENCES...?

A POLICE CAR MIGHT COME IN HANDY HERE...

TRACTORS ARE A USEFUL PART OF THE TEAM...

SUBMARINES EXPLORE A WATERY WORLD!

CAN YOU SPOT THE 9 DIFFERENCES...?

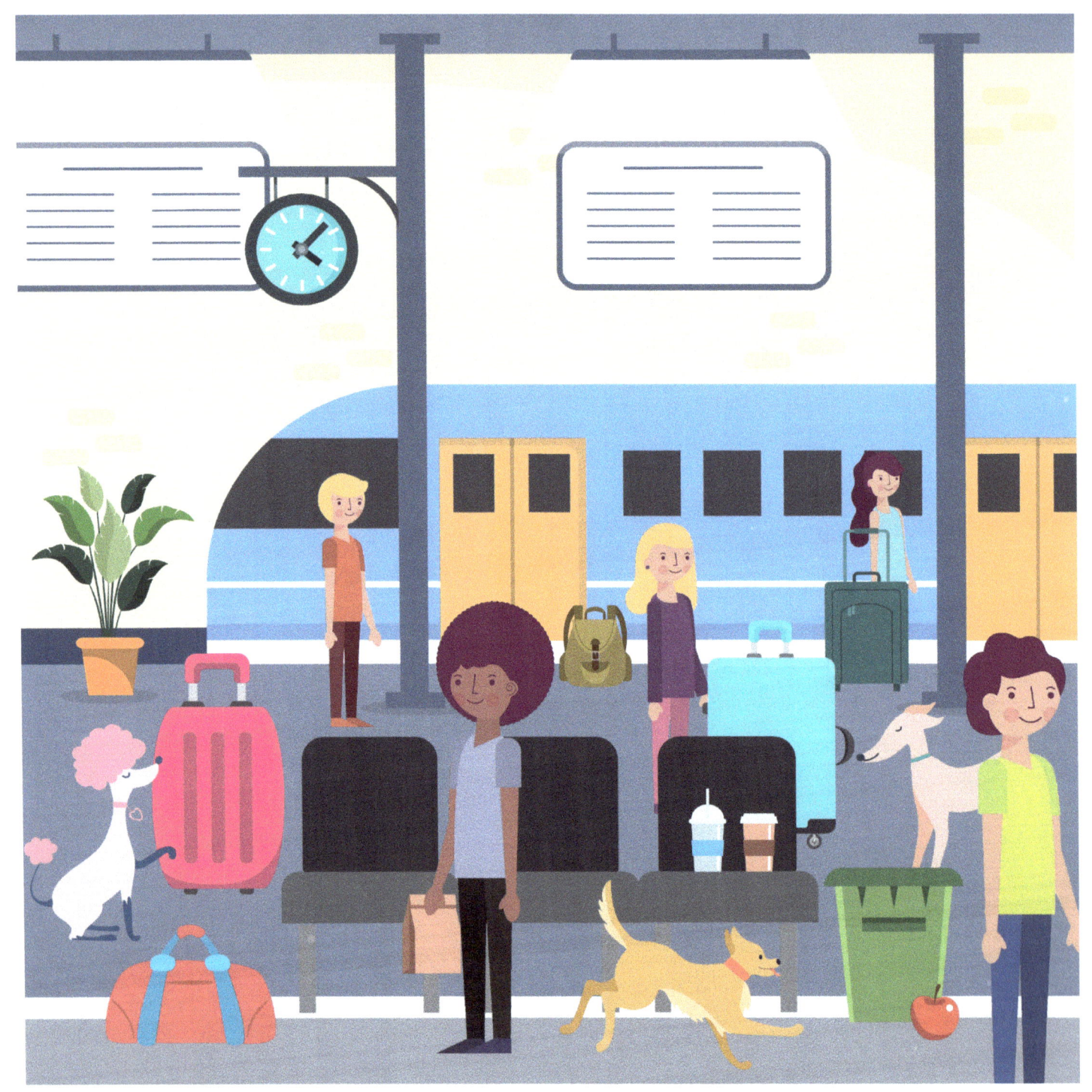

IT'S TIME TO TRAVEL ON THE CITY TRAIN!

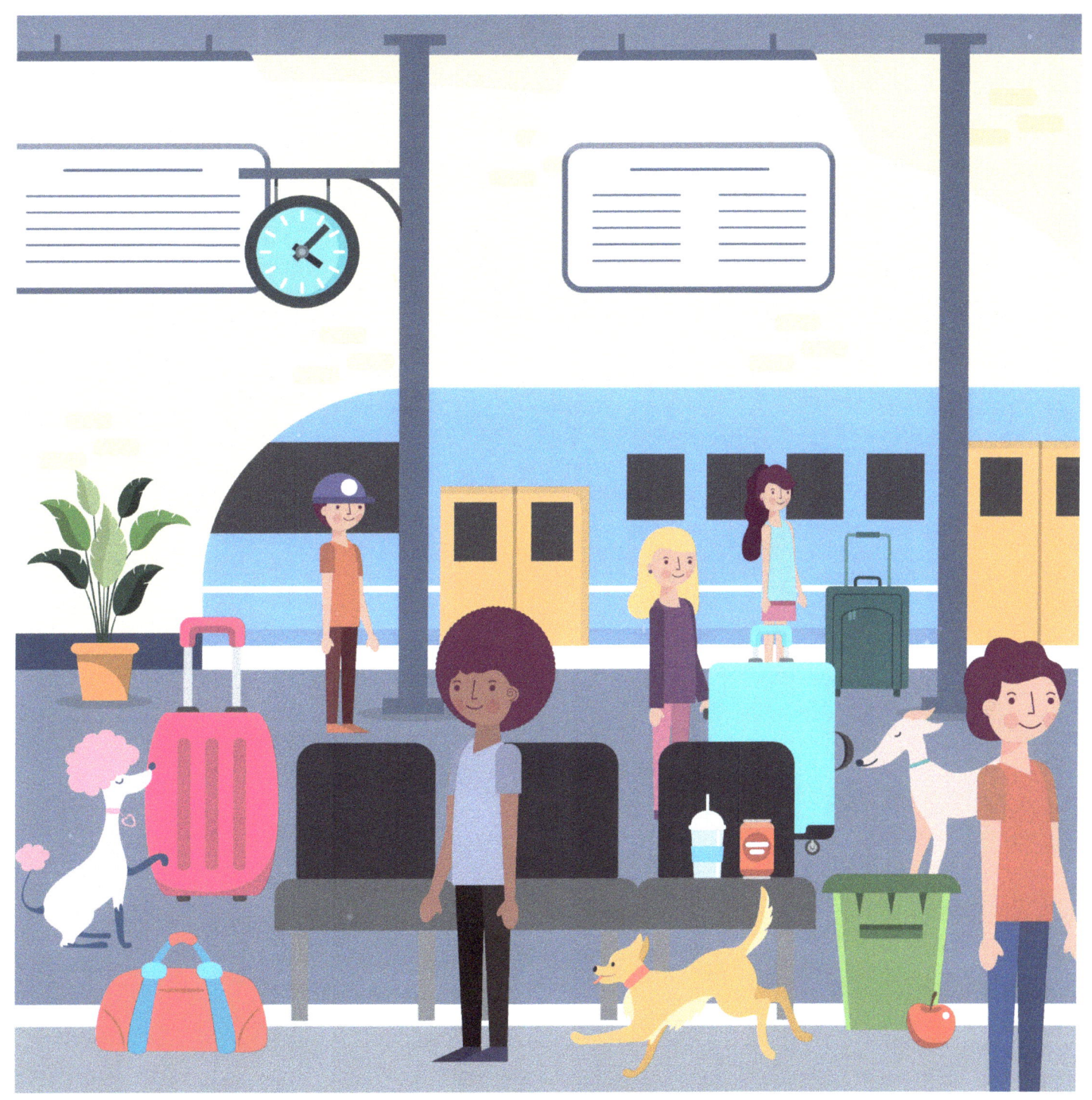

THE FINAL PUZZLE... THANKS FOR PLAYING!

CAN YOU SPOT THE 10 DIFFERENCES...?

ANSWERS!

Check to see how many differences you found!

THE END!

BESTSELLERS!

Type the unique number in the Amazon search bar... **and it'll take you right to it!**

1980596743

1973102145

1728837782

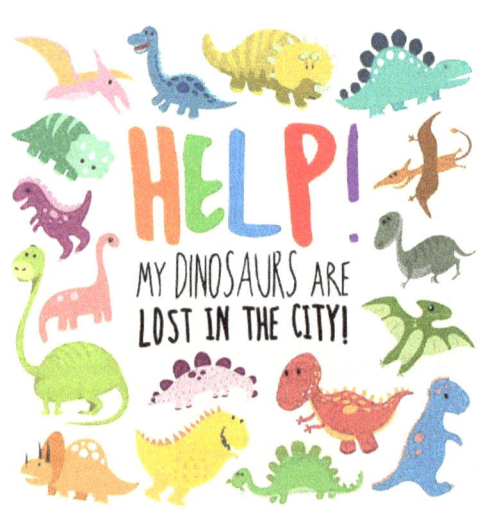

1976776511

1724117491

1549977660

BESTSELLERS!

Type the unique number in the Amazon search bar... **and it'll take you right to it!**

1914047133

1914047060

1914047079

1914047125

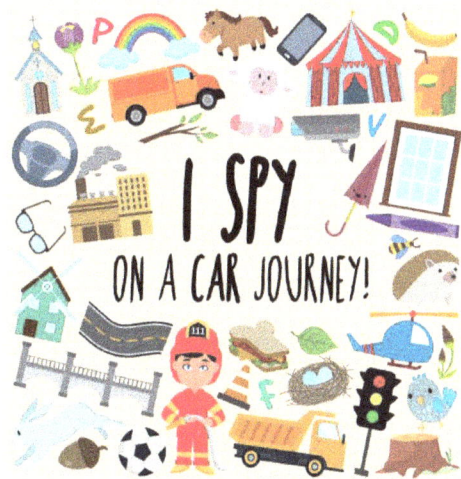

B096X7H7P4

1914047087

www.ingramcontent.com/pod-product-compliance
Lightning Source LLC
Chambersburg PA
CBHW051321110526
44590CB00031B/4434